SCHUBERT

Mass in G

For voices, strings and organ,
with optional wind and timpani.
Arranged for SSA

by Michael Pilkington

Order no: NOV 200201

NOVELLO PUBLISHING LIMITED

The piano reduction by Berthold Tours has been revised to reflect Schubert's scoring for strings and organ, and to enable the work to be performed with piano alone.

This arrangement is based on the Novello edition of 1977 which restores the original words for the four inner movements. A full score and orchestral parts for the 1977 edition, which are compatable with this arrangement, are available on hire.

ORCHESTRATION

2 Oboes or Clarinets in C *(optional)*
2 Bassoons *(optional)*

2 Trumpets in D *(optional)*

Timpani *(optional)*

Strings

Organ

© Copyright 1997 Novello & Company Ltd.
Published in Great Britain by Novello Publishing Limited
Head Office: 14-15 Berners Street, London W1T 3LJ
Tel +44 (0)20 7612 7400   Fax +44 (0)20 7612 7546
Sales and Hire:
Music Sales Distribution Centre, Newmarket Road, Bury St Edmunds, Suffolk IP33 3YB
Tel +44 (0)1284 702600   Fax +44 (0)1284 768301
Web: www.chesternovello.com   e-mail: music@musicsales.co.uk

MASS IN G

Arranged for SSA
by Michael Pilkington

1. Kyrie eleison

Franz Schubert
1797–1828

2. Gloria in excelsis

12

3. Credo

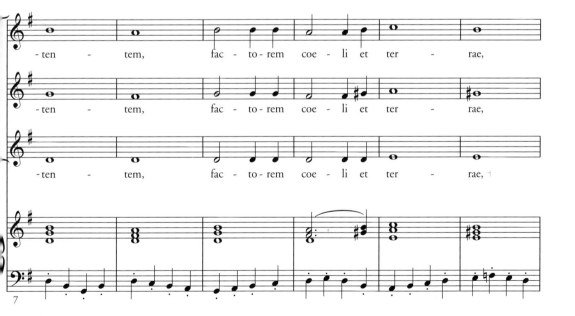

49

55

61

pas - sus, et se - pul - tus est.

pas - sus, et se - pul - tus est.

pas - sus, et se - pul - tus est.

f legato

85

91

D *ff*

Et re - sur - rex - it ter - ti - a di - e, se -

Et re - sur - rex - it ter - ti - a di - e, se -

Et re - sur - rex - it ter - ti - a di - e, se -

D

ff

97

sae - cu - li, et vi - tam ven - tu - ri sae - cu - li.

sae - cu - li, et vi - tam ven - tu - ri sae - cu - li.

sae - cu - li, et vi - tam ven - tu - ri sae - cu - li.

176

A - men, A - men, A - men, A - men.

A - men, A - men, A - men, A - men.

A - men, A - men, A - men, A - men.

182

4. Sanctus

5. Benedictus

be - ne - dic - tus in no - mi - ne Do - mi -

be - ne - dic - tus in no - mi - ne Do - mi -

qui ve - nit in no - mi - ne Do - mi -

fz   *cresc.*

46

-ni, qui ve - nit in

-ni, be - ne - dic - tus qui ve - nit in

-ni, qui ve - nit in

f   *p*   *f*   *p*

48

no - mi - ne Do - mi - ni.

no - mi - ne Do - mi - ni.

no - mi - ne Do - mi - ni.

pp

50

40

san - na in_ ex - cel - sis, O - san - na, O - san - na in ex - cel -

cel - sis, O - san - na_ in ex - cel - sis, O - san - na in ex - cel -

san - na in ex - cel - sis,_ O - san - na in ex - cel - sis, in ex - cel -

65

C

ff

-sis, O - san - na in ex - cel - sis, O - san - na in ex -

ff

-sis, O - san - na in ex - cel - sis, O - san - na in ex -

ff

-sis, O - san - na in ex - cel - sis, O - san - na in ex -

C

ff

70

6. Agnus Dei

ALTO SOLO

Ag - nus De - i, qui tol - lis pecca - ta mun-di, mi - se-re-re no - bis,

mi - se - re - re no - bis,

B FULL

mi - se-re-re no - bis, mi - se - re, mi - se - re

mi - se-re-re no - bis, mi - se - re, mi - se - re

mi - se-re no - bis, mi - se - re, mi - se - re, mi - se - re

Printed in England by Caligraving Limited Thetford Norfolk

2 3 4 5 6 7 8 9